WELCOME TO THE WORLD OF ANIMALS

Whales

Diane Swanson

Gareth Stevens Publishing
MILWAUKEE

For a free color catalog describing Gareth Stevens' list of high-quality books and multimedia programs, call 1-800-542-2595 (USA) or 1-800-461-9120 (Canada). Gareth Stevens Publishing's Fax: (414) 225-0377. See our catalog, too, on the World Wide Web: http://gsinc.com

The publishers acknowledge the support of the Canada Council for the Arts and the Cultural Services Branch of the Government of British Columbia in making this publication possible.

Library of Congress Cataloging-in-Publication Data

Swanson, Diane, 1944-
    [Welcome to the world of whales]
    Whales / by Diane Swanson.
        p. cm. — (Welcome to the world of animals)
    Originally published: Welcome to the world of whales. North Vancouver, B.C.:
Whitecap Books, © 1996.
    Includes index.
    Summary: Describes the physical characteristics and behaviors of these large
mammals which live in water.
    ISBN 0-8368-2216-1 (lib. bdg.)
    1. Whales—Juvenile literature. [1. Whales.] I. Title. II. Series: Swanson, Diane,
1944- Welcome to the world of animals.
    QL737.C4S785   1998
    599.5—dc21   98-6598

This North American edition first published in 1998 by
Gareth Stevens Publishing
1555 North RiverCenter Drive, Suite 201
Milwaukee, WI 53212 USA

This U.S. edition © 1998 by Gareth Stevens, Inc. Original edition © 1996 by Diane Swanson. First published in 1996 by Whitecap Books, Vancouver/Toronto. Additional end matter © 1998 by Gareth Stevens.

Gareth Stevens series editor: Dorothy L. Gibbs
Editorial assistant: Diane Laska
Cover design: Renee M. Bach

Cover photograph: Victoria Hurst/First Light
Photo credits: Flip Nicklin/First Light 4, 8, 18, 26; Natural Selection/First Light 6, 28; D. Cheeseman/First Light 10; Bavaria/First Light 12; C. Allan Morgan/First Light 14, 30; Thomas Kitchin/First Light 16, 22, 24; Michael Baytoff/First Light 20.

Printed in Mexico

1 2 3 4 5 6 7 8 9 02 01 00 99 98

Contents

World of Difference

Wild and wet, whales are giants. The biggest is the blue whale. It is longer than a basketball court and as heavy as a hundred cars. Besides being the biggest whale, it is also the biggest animal in the world.

Other giants include the fin whale and the sperm whale. The fin whale is almost as long as the blue whale but not as wide. The sperm whale is the shortest giant — only about as long as three cars — but its head alone is the length of one car. Even most dolphins and porpoises, which are types of small whales, grow at least as large as a man.

This giant fin whale has come to the surface to breathe through the two side-by-side blowholes in its head.

Whales come in different colors, including gray, gray-blue, black, and white. Some are colored in patches. Others are spotted or speckled.

Although whales swim and live in the ocean, they are not fish. Whales are mammals, warm-blooded animals — just like people. They cannot

The bottle-nosed dolphin is a whale with a built-in smile.

breathe underwater. No matter how deep they dive, they always return to the surface for air.

At the surface, whales spew stale air out of nostrils, called blowholes, in the tops of their heads. This spray of air looks like your breath on a cold day. Whales that have teeth each have one blowhole; toothless whales have two blowholes.

Before whales dive underwater, they gulp huge breaths of fresh air. Then they hold the air in, or hold their breath, by keeping their blowholes closed.

WONDER WHALES

Whales are amazing! Here are just a few of the reasons why:

- Sperm whales can hold their breath for up to two hours.

- During its first year of life, a gray whale can gain more than 1 pound (½ kilogram) an hour.

- The Atlantic white-sided dolphin has 120 to 132 teeth. Adult humans have only 32.

- The tongue of a blue whale can weigh as much as an elephant.

Where in the World

The watery world of whales is the sea. Whales travel all Earth's oceans. Some prefer deep water; others prefer shallow. A few whales also swim in rivers and lakes.

Different kinds of whales live in the different types of waters along the coasts of North America. Narwhals and belugas live along the icy northern coast of the Arctic. Some kinds of dolphins and porpoises live only along the Pacific coast; others, only along the Atlantic coast. The fin; sperm; blue; humpback; and killer whales, called orcas, swim in both the Atlantic and Pacific oceans — and in parts of the Arctic Ocean.

Bottle-nosed dolphins travel in a group to search for food in shallow water.

9

With its tail up, the humpback whale dives down. It is exploring its summer home in cold seas.

At one time, gray whales lived along both the Pacific and Atlantic coasts; today, they are found only in the Pacific. Like many whales, gray whales travel north each summer to feast in arctic waters. In winter, they head for warm Mexican waters. They mate there and, about twelve months later, give birth. This yearly journey, or migration, is one of the longest made by any mammal in the world.

When traveling whales get tired, they take short naps. Sometimes they float with their backs just above the surface of the water. From time to time, they raise their sleepy heads to breathe, then drop them down again.

Earth's oceans used to have many more whales swimming in them — especially blue, sperm, and humpback whales. Today, only gray whales living along the Pacific coast survive in their past numbers.

HOW WHALES EVOLVED

Some scientists believe that whales once lived on land — millions of years ago — and were large, furry animals that walked on four legs.

Gradually, these land animals became sea creatures. Their fur coats, which made swimming difficult, disappeared. They put on fat, called blubber, to keep them warm in cold seas. Their back legs vanished, and their front legs became flippers. To make breathing easier, their nostrils moved to the tops of their heads.

World of the Strainer

Most whales that do not have teeth, such as blue, fin, gray, and humpback whales, use baleen to strain their food out of seawater. These whales, called baleen whales, have hundreds of long, thin baleen plates hanging from their upper jaws. Baleen feels like fingernails, except one edge of each plate is bristly.

To eat, a baleen whale fills its huge mouth with seawater. Each mouthful contains thousands of small sea creatures, including shrimplike animals called krill. When the whale forces the seawater back out of its mouth, the baleen traps the prey,

A cluster of snouts pokes through the water; the humpback whales are feeding.

13

A gray whale's baleen is the shortest. It is only 1 foot (30 cm) long. Some whales have baleen twelve times longer.

and the whale scrapes it off with its tongue. Sometimes, whales herd krill close together before feeding so each big mouthful brims with food.

In arctic summers, krill group together so thickly they make the sea look reddish brown. When the blue whale comes to feed, it gobbles up forty million krill a day. Like the fin whale and other krill-feeders, the blue whale has pleats, or folds, of skin over its throat and chest. These pleats expand so the whale can take in a lot of water and food at one time.

Most baleen whales strain the surface of the sea, but gray whales feed along the bottom. They strain out water, sand, and mud and swallow shrimp, clams, and fish. Sometimes, to make a meal, they force water out of their mouths to stir up the seafloor, then gulp down the animals that rise.

From top to bottom, the sea is worth the strain for baleen whales!

FISHING WITH BUBBLES

Humpback whales sometimes use bubbles to catch fish. They puff air from their blowholes underwater. The air rises and forms a floating net of bubbles.

Flapping their flippers and blaring like trumpets, the humpback whales herd small fish toward the bubble net. Then up shoot the whales. With mouths wide open and throats fully stretched, they snatch the trapped fish, strain out the water, and gulp down their catch.

World of the Hunter

Most whales that have teeth use them for hunting, but their teeth are built for grabbing and holding prey, not biting and chewing it. Sperm whales, belugas, porpoises, and dolphins (including killer whales) usually swallow food whole. Whales that feed on larger prey, such as seals, swallow it in chunks.

Keen hearing helps whales hunt in dark, cloudy waters, but their ears are not easy to find. They are inside the whale's head, and the openings to the inner ears are no bigger than a match tip. Still, a whale hears very well — much better than it sees or smells.

Killer whales are speedy hunters. Sometimes they travel as fast as racehorses.

Kings once traded gold for cups made from narwhal teeth. They believed the teeth were magical.

When a killer whale senses a seal lying on some ice above it, the whale charges to the surface. Bursting through the ice, it flings the seal into the sea and grabs it.

Whales have strong tail muscles to help them swim well and chase prey. Whales swim by pumping their tail fins, called flukes, up and down. They use their armlike flippers to steer.

Some kinds of whales, such as killer whales, hunt in teams. Large teams, called pods, might have hundreds of whales. The pod is a whale's family.

The whales in a pod whack the water with their heads and tails to scare fish and herd them together. Then the pod forms a circle around the fish. One by one, each whale zooms into the circle and grabs some prey. In the world of the hunter, even young whales eat well.

LONG IN THE TOOTH

Imagine having a tooth more than half the length of your body! A male narwhal about 16 feet (5 meters) long can grow a tooth about 10 feet (3 m) long. Females might grow a long tooth, too, but they rarely do.

The tooth is coiled like a corkscrew and sticks out through the narwhal's top lip. It usually is the narwhal's only tooth.

Narwhals grab prey with their jaws, so their tooth probably is not used for hunting. It might, however, help a narwhal attract a mate.

World of Words

Trills, barks, squeals, and squeaks — all whales make sounds. In their huge ocean homes, talking helps whales keep track of each other. It also helps them find their way and find their prey.

Whales that have teeth make sounds, then listen for the sounds to bounce back, or echo. Echoes help the whales learn the size and shape of another animal. They also help the whales decide how far away the animal is and in which direction it is moving.

Each pod of killer whales speaks a language of its own. About twelve different

Every year, male humpback whales change the songs they sing — just a little.

calls help these whales stay in contact with each other and work together. When one pod talks to another pod, the whales often shriek like sirens.

Some scientists do not think baleen whales, such as humpback whales, listen for echoes, but these whales still make many sounds. Some sigh

Beluga whales "talk" the most. Sometimes they sound like children shouting.

softly; others sing loudly. Male humpback whales sing louder than any other animal on Earth. Their songs seem to be the most well known.

Humpback whales sing love songs to attract female whales. They sing scary songs to frighten other males. They sing traveling songs to contact each other. Some of their songs last thirty minutes, and the whales sing them again and again.

Along the coast, the humpbacks swim far apart, so their traveling songs are like long-distance calls that help them keep in touch.

A WHALE OF A CANARY

Belugas sing, whistle, and chirp, so early whale hunters named them "sea canaries." Sometimes, hundreds of belugas all sing together — like a giant canary choir.

Belugas make so many sounds that they could have many names. You could call them "sea dogs," because they bark and yip. You could also call them "sea cows," because they moo, too.

Some of their sounds have special meanings. Belugas seem to moan when they are afraid and trill when they are happy.

New World

Most whales come into the world tail first. As soon as baby whales, called calves, are born, their mothers help them swim to the surface of the sea. At the surface, the calves open their blowholes and take in their first breath of air.

Newborn whale calves are huge. A killer whale weighs about 400 pounds (180 kg) at birth. A blue whale weighs about a ton.

Whale calves are born hungry. They demand food right away. A calf might push its mother with its head and press against her stomach to be fed. A mother whale

Killer whales are family animals. They travel, hunt, and play as families all year round.

25

A humpback whale feeds her calf about forty times a day. Humpback whales might live as long as seventy years.

feeds her calf the rich, creamy milk she makes in her body. She must feed it again and again. Fortunately, mother whales usually have only one calf at a time.

Depending on the kind of whale, calves feed from their mothers for six to twenty-four months. All that time, the mothers — and some "baby-sitting" aunts — protect the calves from dangers, such as hungry sharks. The calves grow fast and put on thick layers of blubber, which help keep them warm.

When they are not feeding, whale calves practice swimming, holding their breath, and diving. They also take time to play.

A calf naps close beside its mother, resting its sleepy head against her. The calf might try to climb on top of its mother, but whales are slippery, and the calf soon slides off.

EARLY LEARNER

Right after it takes its first breath, a newborn killer whale starts to practice swimming. It stays close to its mother as it moves back and forth underwater. The calf is able to hold its breath until it returns to the surface, but, there, it coughs and sputters. Breathing is something to practice, too.

The newborn soon learns to talk. Like a human baby, it learns by listening to its family. Then it copies the whistles and clicks that fill its world.

Fun World

Playing in the water is fun. Whales like it, too. Dolphins like to leap over waves — even waves made by ships as they cross the sea. That game, however, can be dangerous. If the dolphin is not careful, it might collide with the ship.

Some whales prefer quieter games. They push and toss shells, seaweed, and almost anything else that floats. One big sperm whale was even seen "sailing" a wooden plank.

Whale calves play a lot. They swim, dive, leap, and splash. For safety, calves usually play near their mothers. Sometimes,

Playful dolphins burst out of the sea. Some do somersaults before splashing down again.

29

A humpback whale leaps to shake tiny animals off its body — and, sometimes, just to have fun.

they even play with their mothers. Gray whale families, for example, have fun rubbing against each other.

Besides being fun, playing is great exercise. It helps whale calves grow strong and healthy. Yet, if a mother whale thinks her calf is playing too hard, she holds it close to her with her flippers until the calf settles down a little.

Adult whales play, too. Killer whales like diving together. Sometimes they turn around suddenly and start chasing each other.

Grown belugas have a game they play over and over. One beluga dives to the seafloor and comes back with a rock on its head. Other belugas push the whale until the rock slides off. Then another beluga dives for a rock and starts the game again.

PEOPLE PLAYMATES

The sea is a whale's playground, but human visitors have sometimes been caught in the games. For example, a particular humpback whale liked to swim close to the sides of ships. When passengers gathered on deck to see it, the whale sprayed their faces!

Dolphins often swim with scuba divers. Swooping up, down, or around — they do whatever the divers do. The more they play, the more they chatter, surrounding divers with chirps and clicks.

Glossary

baleen — the bony plates that hang in rows from the upper jaw of a toothless whale and are used to strain food out of seawater.

blowhole — an opening at the top of a whale's head that is used for breathing.

blubber — the fat on a whale.

evolve — to change form gradually over a long period of time.

flipper — the armlike part of a whale, or some other sea mammal, that is used for swimming.

fluke — one of the finlike parts at the end of a whale's tail.

krill — tiny, shrimplike animals that are the main food of baleen whales.

pleat — (n) a flat, even fold of overlapping material.

pod — a large group of animals, such as whales.

snout — the part of an animal's face that sticks out in front and includes the animal's nose and mouth.

trill — (v) to make a quivering sound.

Index